What Can Live in a
Desert?

D0061599

by Sheila Anderson

first step nonfiction

Lerner Publications Company · Minneapolis

A desert is a habitat.

It is where plants and
animals live.

Animals have special **adaptations**.

These help them live in the desert.

Foxes have large ears that
send out heat to help them
6 keep cool.

Gerbils have brown **coats** that match the color of sand.

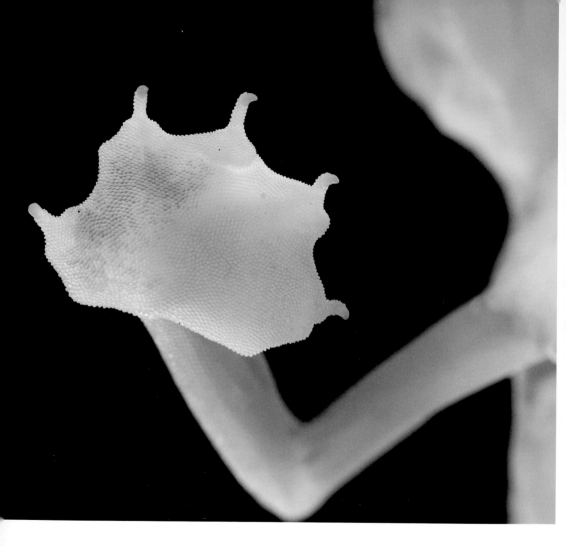

Desert geckos have **webbed** feet.

They can walk on top of
sand without sinking.

Jackrabbits have long legs.

These help them outrun
hunters.

Scorpions grab insects with their **pincers**.

They kill their **prey** with their tails.

Roadrunners have long legs.

They can run from danger
or chase dinner.

This snake's skin is the same
color as the sand.

What other adaptations help animals live in the desert?

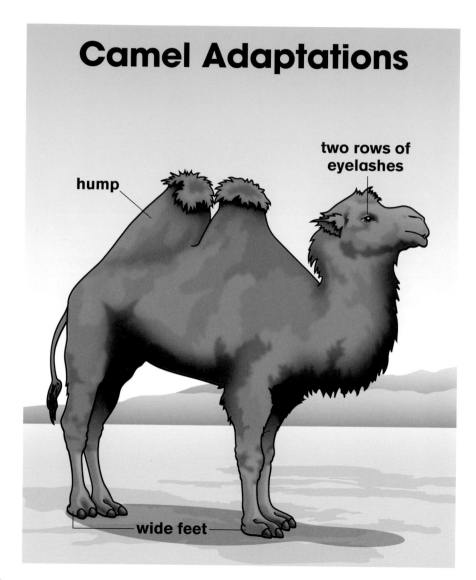

Camel Adaptations

two rows of eyelashes

hump

wide feet

Learn More about Adaptations

Camels store fat in humps on their backs. They use the fat for energy when they can't find food. Camels have two rows of eyelashes on each eye. They keep sand out of the camel's eyes. Camels use flat, wide feet to walk on sand without sinking in. Neat!

Fun Facts

 Some desert snakes swim through the sand. This is because the sand below the surface is cooler than the sand on top.

 Some desert lizards hop so they have less contact with hot sand.

 Kangaroo rats only come out at night, when the temperature is cooler.

 Rattlesnakes sleep deeply during the winter, when deserts can be cold.

Cactus wrens make nests on cactuses. Tough, scaly skin on their legs keeps them from being poked by the cactus's spines.

 Rattlesnakes have rattles on the ends of their tails. They shake the rattles to scare off hunters.

 The coats of coyotes and mountain lions are the color of the desert.

Glossary

adaptations – things that help a plant or animal live in a specific habitat

coats – layers of fur

pincers – claws that look like scissors

prey – an animal that is hunted and eaten by other animals

webbed – connected by a fold of skin

Index

coats – 7

color – 7, 16

ears – 6

legs – 10, 14

pincers – 12

skin – 16

tails – 13

webbed feet – 8

The images in this book are used with the permission of: © David Watson/Dreamstime.com, p. 2; © Rinusbaak/Dreamstime.com, p. 3; © Yuri Gupta/Dreamstime.com, pp. 4, 22 (first from top); © Stefan Mokrzecki/SuperStock, p. 5; © age fotostock/SuperStock, pp. 6, 13, 14, 17; © Louise Murray/Alamy, pp. 7, 22 (second from top); © Solvin Zankl/Visuals Unlimited, Inc., pp. 8, 22 (fifth from top); © Mauritius/SuperStock, pp. 9, 12, 22 (third from top); U.S. Fish and Wildlife Service, pp. 10, 22 (fourth from top); © John E. Marriott/Alamy, p. 11; © Joe McDonald/Visuals Unlimited, Inc., p. 15; © Heinrich van der Berg/Gallo Images/Getty Images, p. 16; © Laura Westlund/Independent Picture Service, p. 18.

Cover: © François De Ribaucourt/Dreamstime.com.

Lerner Publications Company
A division of Lerner Publishing Group, Inc.
241 First Avenue North
Minneapolis, MN 55401 USA

For reading levels and more information, look up this title at www.lernerbooks.com.

Library of Congress Cataloging-in-Publication Data

Anderson, Sheila.
     What can live in a desert? / by Sheila Anderson.
       p.   cm. — (First step nonfiction. Animal adaptations)
     Includes index.
     ISBN 978–0–7613–4570–1 (lib. bdg. : alk. paper)
     ISBN 978–0–7613–6254–8 (eBook)
     1. Desert animals—Adaptation—Juvenile literature. I. Title.
   QL116.A53 2011
   591.754—dc22   2009024857

Manufactured in the United States of America
3 – PC – 8/1/14